MW01015779

f.

Love Is What You Are Made Of

Written and illustrated by

A.M. Perry

Balboa Press books may be ordered through booksellers or by contacting:

Balboa Press
A Division of Hay House
1663 Liberty Drive
Bloomington, IN 47403
www.balboapress.com
1 (877) 407-4847

ISBN: 978-1-4525-2247-0 (sc)
ISBN: 978-1-4525-2248-7 (e)

Library of Congress Control Number: 2014916829

Printed in the United States of America.

Balboa Press rev. date: 11/18/2014

BALBOA
PRESS
A DIVISION OF HAY HOUSE

For my Taran and Sascha,

who taught me how to love.

On a vast rolling ocean sparkling blue,
In a brown wooden boat sat wonderful you.

Great big eyes stared at the sun above,
Asking "Oh, just *what* am I made of?"

A question that shot up into the stars,

Drifted through the *Milky Way*,

Landing on space dust - somewhere near Mars.

Until the w i n d picked up and blew it away...

It soared around upon a breeze,

Then hid in the feathers of a wise young owl,

Who was sailing across the seven seas.

Oh, just what am I made of?

H, OH, OH

What, What, What

What am I made of?

Sunsets in your heart of gold ,

But that is not all that you behold -

Smiles bounding from ear to ear,

Dance upon those cute little lips that I love so dear.

SMILES

sunsets

Beauty is in every part of you,

Your eyes, your toes and your spirit too.

beauty

You are made of laughter, so laugh out loud,

And of yourself, be

Oh

So

Proud.

Now courage and patience you surely keep,
Chasing dreams even in your sleep.

You are made of confidence, this I know

Trusting in yourself as you grow, grow, grow.

confidence

TRUST

Inside of you shines a colorful beam,

Because you are also made of every

Bright rainbow's dream.

rainbows

The sound of your name brings peace to my heart,

For I have *loved* you right from the start.

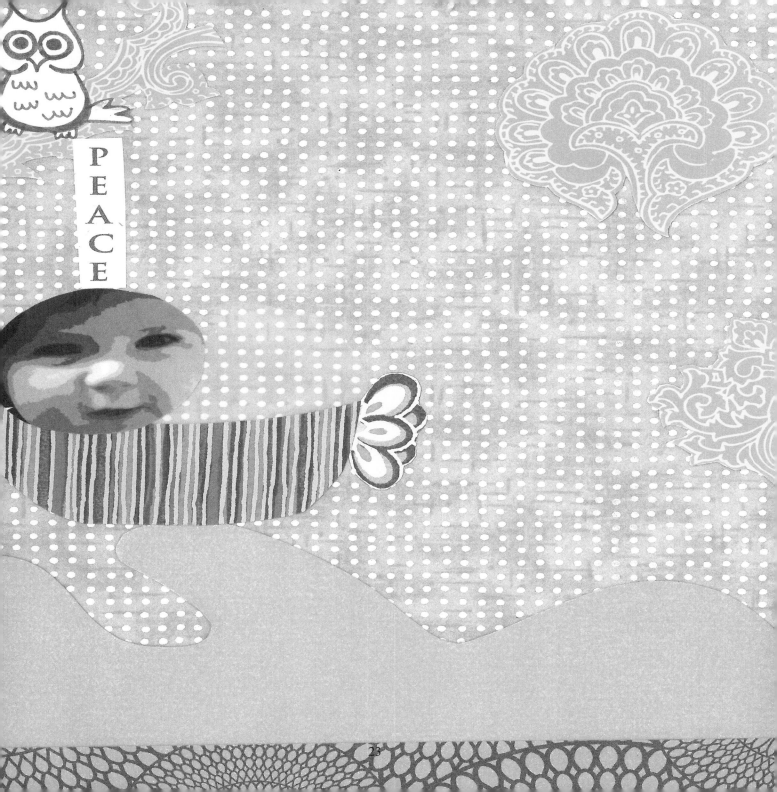

PEACE

Comfort for any low days that may come,

Gentle h u g s to remind you of where you come from.

comfort

hugs

For in our hearts you will find a space,

And where you belong is just that place.

So to answer your question,

Love, my dear,

Love is what you are made of.

Love

Love

Love

CPSIA information can be obtained at www.ICGtesting.com
Printed in the USA
LVOW01s1824011214

416533LV00001B/2/P